To Mike,

Thank you for
giving my words
a voice!

Jay Cruz

Timeless Chatter
Between the Heart and Mind

a collection of poetry and prose by

Jay Long

For my Mother

My steady ground to stand on, the hand that lifts me up, no matter what fall I may have taken and the wind that allows me to soar.

INTRODUCTION

Poetry, as it's defined in the modern dictionary, is a literary work in which special intensity is given to the expression of feelings and ideas by the use of distinctive style and rhythm. The definition is pretty accurate. The written word, when by itself, is simple and sometimes holds no meaning whatsoever, but when certain words are grouped together, it can be magical. The beauty of poetry is that for every reader, the meaning may be completely different. Poetry, more so than other forms of writing, allows the reader to escape, to relate their own experiences to the words the writer has bled onto the page. Readers connect to the poet and on some level, the two become intimate partners, even if for a short time. Our hearts and minds always seem to be at odds with each other. It's an endless struggle of thoughts and feelings. Timeless Chatter Between the Heart and Mind is a collection of writings that seems to capture that.

Denial

It was a Sunday, at 2:30 in the morning, when the fighting and denial stopped. I had fought it every second, of every minute, of every hour, of every day, leading up to that moment. I wanted it to get lost in the tangled web and skeletons deep within me. Not because I was afraid, but because I knew you'd wreck me in the most beautiful way possible. The scars on my heart peeled themselves back and started beating freely once again, again. But with every 'I Love You' my heart shouted, my mind whispered, 'but you can't wait forever.'

My Home

You are not the end to my beginning
Or a tender love song my soul sings
You are my first wish
My earliest dream
The beat my heart was given
  when I took my first breath
My destiny
My fate
My home

Beauty of You

The sun isn't brighter.
The moon isn't higher.
The sky isn't bluer, nor are the oceans any
  more powerful.
But with you in my life,
I simply notice all the beauty in the world.

Moonshine

The moon could not keep us to itself
For a love like ours wouldn't be
   held captive in the shadows.
Embraced by the sun, we shined for
   all to see.

Heartbeats & Forever

When I hear of heartbeats and soft whispers,
I picture a warm mid-summer rain hitting
a tin roof as the wind blows off the lake
and caresses the weary bodies of long time
lovers. When I'm told about eyes that sparkle
and smiles that run from ear to ear, I see a
star filled spring night, with endless
dreamers allowing the moon to shine down
on only them. And when I hear of forever, the
only thing I can see is you.

The Answer

As the warm fire lit the room around us, I sat
and stared into her endless eyes. So many
questions of lost love came to mind and I
asked,
"'How does one see the light, when their life
is spent in the darkness?'
'When each rose touched has left a scar, how
can one love so freely?'
'When each waking moment is a nightmare,
how can dreams come true?'
'And how can I be truly free, when the walls I
built have not crumbled to the ground?' "
She held my hands in hers as if they were a
precious treasure she'd been searching for
since her heart first learned to beat. Her
answer came with all the knowledge and
wisdom of a lifetime. She looked at me
and said, 'you simply believe."

Darkness in Waiting

Dusk creeps in without warning

leaving me alone,
longing for the moon's kiss

My gypsy soul
never seems to find itself still
for I am a child of the night
I am best hidden in the shadows

The darkness pulls at my wings
unlocking the shackles of self doubt
forever breaking the chains
  that have kept me from soaring

And I am free

Fading Eternity

The moons
The stars
The sun
all laugh at us

They have seen millions of days
and countless lovers lose hope
   in tomorrow's dream

A cracked smile they wear
   for every FOREVER they hear whispered

They wager with our wishes
how quickly the end will come

For they know true love isn't formed on the
   tail of a dying star
It is built each day for eternity

Masterpiece

Our canvas was brought to life with laughter
and love
Now the hands that once held you so tightly
are left picking up the pieces of a broken
masterpiece

Stars and Moonlight

Countless stars in the night sky have heard
your name whispered in wishes. There are
full moons that have yet to shine on your
midnight kisses. And one beating heart that
will always be yours.

Whiskey Night

As I take a bite
  out of the midnight sky
I can feel my blood
  begin to grow cold
Just another whiskey night
  without you
And no matter how much spills
  across my tongue
I can't get the taste
  of your lips out of my mouth

I Will

One day I will be at peace with myself
I will whisper to the world that I am
  here now with no plans on leaving
I will see that each memory I made
  has built the mountain I am standing on
  and the flames of each bridge I burned lit
  the way

Today

The sunshine casts your shadow on me
Shielding my eyes
Allowing me to see all of your beauty
Today is a good day
And should the rains come,
  to take away our happiness
Know I will stand as your shelter
  against the storm
Today is a good day

Wandering

Somewhere in the distance
  off the beaten path of life
  lies our true existence
So many stumble down the road
  never knowing where the next turn
  will lead them
Take the time to find your center
Journey with purpose
For nothing good
  will ever come from wandering

Seek the Beat

When I close my eyes to the night,
it feels as if my heart leaves my body
seeking its beat. It's been lost since
the moment you said goodbye. Rattling
around in its cage, behind flesh and
bone. Dreams try to keep it safe, as
falling wishes scream across the night
sky. And there you are, a picture perfect
memory holding out your hand, asking me to
leap. And just as we start to soar hand in
hand, the morning air fills my lungs once
again and you are gone.

Artful Dodger

His love was
  an artful dodger.
His heart
  had a way of running
  from the fire,
  never allowing another
  to match its beat

Pinky Promise

She said 'I love you', like it was a question
she had to ask herself. And before her mind
could give her the answer, I kissed her. Open
mouthed, under the light of a crescent moon
that had been following us all night, like our
own personal chaperon. When our lips finally
parted, she looked in my eyes and said 'I love
you' again, like it was a pinky promise
between her heart and mine.

Fire & Light

She set fire to each bridge
  that ever left her lost
Scorched every path
  she stumbled down while finding
  her way to happiness
The one way dead end roads
  no longer her destination
Instead, she breathed fire
  to light her way

Dead Ends

The walls have crumbled
The space has been filled
  with bullshit and fluff
We weren't what love is.
We tried to be what everyone
  thinks is love
I'm not here to be fixed,
So I do you no good
I'm not here to babysit a soul,
  that won't allow love in.
I won't slam my heart into empty spaces
I felt like I was on display
Like you were window shopping
  and I was on the clearance rack
I thought I could never walk this world
  without your light
Until I realized you were just
  leading me down one way dead end streets

Moonrise

At the end of the day she spread her love
across the sky like stars. Each one holding
a piece of magic. The twinkles matched her
heartbeat and the moon rose in her eyes.

Beauty Within

She asked me if I thought she was beautiful
and I told her - 'No'
I touched her face and said, 'beautiful gets
lost in translation, wrapped up by looks and
there just isn't a word big enough to describe
all the beauty you hold within.'

In the Darkness

In the darkness
 of tomorrow's unknown
I will light your way

For every beat my heart holds
Your name will echo

Long after your hand has left mine
I will watch over you

Undaunted

Crashes and kisses
Fumbling fingers
Find their path
Locked in an embrace
Staring into a stranger's face
Soft to the touch
  but hardened in the heart
Afraid to be alone
Afraid to love
Memories and broken dreams
  pave her way home
Undaunted living to her
Madness to some

Something Beautiful

The doors were left opened
The past stretched out for as
  far as the eye could see
The future, although bright,
  was hidden behind walls built
  to keep from ever being blind-sided
Today it's time to let go
Lock those doors
Throw away the key and head out
  to find something beautiful

Dying Beauty

The morning after she left reminded me of
the pulled petals off a rose; still beautiful, but
not complete. I sat in my own tears, afraid to
wake up to the reality of lost love once again.
My heart pounded in its chest, like a raging
animal trying to escape its cage. At that
moment I was thankful for the bones that
formed that cage. Sturdy and thick, they held
captive a heart that once roamed freely like a
gypsy does. Her love tamed the fool that no
one dared to try and settle down. I held my
eyes shut and imagined her touch. I thought
back to the last time our bodies were one;
that night in the rain, alone in the field. We
were like wild horses and our carefree souls
were riding them through the storm. With
each lightning strike our bodies crashed
together like the slamming screen door that
hung on my grandmother's back porch. I
could still smell her perfume on the sheets;
jasmine with a hint of vanilla. I opened my
eyes hoping to find it all a dream and her soft
body lying next to me. But it was too late.
Beauty in any form dies quickly, it never
simply fades away. Just like the pulled petals
off a rose.

He Knew

All he knew of love
 was that it whispered his name
  from across the bar
  when the whiskey was gone
All he knew of beauty
  was what he was told he'd never be
All he knew of loss
   was everything

Rising Chaos

In the darkness
I press your skin against my lips
So that I know I am home
Always the angel
Forever a saint
I'll be your sinner
When the heavens come to judge
Let the mercy of your touch
Leave me in the stunning chaos
   of the moon rising in your eyes

Lessons Learned

Each of her goodbyes held a lesson
Painful teachings of lost love
One by one
They sent me down a predestined path
Had I only known
I'd of broken the cycle
Chose my direction better
I didn't need the knowledge
  of a broken heart
Or the constant screaming
  of a tormented mind
Instead
I would have swallowed that first hello
I would have bitten my tongue
  to hold back the words
Tasted the blood in my mouth for a moment
Rather than cough it up
Each time her name is whispered

Life

Life passes us by each and every day. During the course of a 24-hour period, we are impacted by the lives of countless others without giving much thought to it. Until one of those lives in nearing or comes to an end.

Our reward for longevity is experiencing the loss of each person close to us over our lifetime. We are blessed with the memories of those who have come into our lives and all those who have ultimately left us. As long as a memory still exists, we never truly leave this world. Where ever Heaven is, I surely hope to find it one day. When my time comes, I hope that all the memories, the smiles the laughs, I have shared and created, carry-on.

The Calling

Behold the red sky
Filled with rage, fury and might
Demons do their deeds
As the souls of angels plunge
  into the depths of the moat
Rattle the cage
To steal all its thunder
For tomorrow is upon us
Judgment day is calling

Give Me Shelter

I could always taste the sunshine's laughter upon your lips. My skin forever tingled under your touch. As I stood in the shadow of your light, I'd get lost in the clouds that fill your mind. No matter where you are tonight, promise me this - when the moon fills the night with hope, wrap me in your wishes and give me shelter inside the twinkle of your bedroom eyes.

Beautiful Madness

I knew her past was full of scars
  but her eyes were filled with hope
Even though the frayed threads of sanity
  barely kept her together
It was her laughter that made me love her
Her shy inappropriate madness
  is what made her beautiful
And the trail of broken pieces she left behind
  her
Let me find my home

Dance With Me

Put your hair up
  so I can see your beauty
Dance with me
  as I lose myself
  in the light of your eyes
Speak to me with your smile
  and bring me home with your kiss

Anointed

I found myself
  staring into the eye of the storm
Alone and jaded
Each bolt of lightning
  shocked my system
  into seeing you were gone
The rumble of the thunder
  shook me to the core
Every raindrop that found my face
  washed me clean again
The heavens were anointing me
  bruised but not broken

Her Kiss

Her lips stole my kiss
Breaking the silence
 of a rainy Sunday night
I could taste the words
  she longed to say
  lingering on my tongue
My eyes caught her stare
  through the clouds and moonlight
I found a girl ready to be loved
  but afraid to let go
A woman filled with dreams
  but a heart still in pieces
And a kiss goodbye
  that somehow saved me

Dance Tonight

Meet me tonight. Dance with me under the
canopy of raindrops that fall down from the
heavens. Let our lips taste the tears of the
angels as they wash our bodies clean.
Embrace the thunder, let it awaken your scar
torn heart, causing it to beat once again. And
in the morning, as the sun splits the sky wide
open, remember the love we have is sought
by countless souls that never share a dance.

The Happening

There's a flash of time just before the sun disappears under the horizon that seems to last an eternity and then in a split second it's gone. We spend so much energy anticipating the finality of it, that we miss the beauty the sunset holds in its entirety. To me that's how most go through life - so focused on the end result, that we miss the details that create the wonders all around us. Half the magic is in the happening. Take the time to cherish those moments.

Slipping Away

As I watched her walk away, I could feel my heart beating in the corners of my mouth. Pounding as if it were trying to break free to chase her. The goodbye lingered on my tongue and felt the world slipping through the palm of my hand. The dryness of my throat caused me to swallow a much needed breath. Instead of tears, my lips parted with a bright smile, for I had known true love and nothing would ever take her memory away.

Love Will Follow

Moments of our lives lost from tirelessly
worrying can never be taken back. Things
that we have no control over steal our joy on
a daily basis, and we allow it. We hold others
opinions of us higher than we hold our own
self worth. To say that we are sometimes our
own worst enemy is an understatement. We
are our only enemy. Our mind constantly
argues with the heart. The heart betrays the
mind. No one can maintain a stable
relationship if the two main parts within us
can't begin to trust one another. Find peace
within your own soul first. Then and only
then, will loving someone not feel like a task
or a chore. Love shouldn't need 'working on'
or a 'building up.' If we could simply learn to
live happily within ourselves, love will
certainly follow.

Her Journey

Though her journey was spent in darkness
She was the light
Her smiles froze time
  causing men to move mountains
Her words rose to the heavens and set in
  stone
Her eyes left questions
  only the bravest would dare seek the
  answers to
Every rose left a scar
  but each heartbeat brought her hope
She was what magic would be if it had a
  breath

Wrapped

There are times when her arms wrap around me like she'll never let me go. It's as if I can feel her body folding into mine. For a brief moment, I forget which one of us is broken. I get lost for a while, until I feel her peeling herself away and she is gone again, leaving me to pick up her pieces.

10-to-1

There are days when the memories won't
ever fade away
As if they are daggers slicing through my
  mind
Images flashing, connecting my yesterday to
  the present
Causing the past to spill into today
Smiles, heartache, joy, pain and love
Rushing back like a dream
That I can't escape
Only to fade
Leaving me
Bleeding

Catch Up

I asked her where she had been all my life.
She smiled and said, 'just waiting for you to
catch up.' From that day I knew my life was
complete and that every wrong turn I took,
had gotten me to the right place.

The Perfect Ending

Under the glow of a corner street light
an old man stares into the darkness
thinking back on his life
the joys he shared
the hearts he broke
the tears he cried
the smiles he couldn't contain
  during moments of pure bliss
thankful for each one
for every choice that turned him down paths
he never thought to take
grasping onto a notebook
each page filled with miles
from days he thought would never end
the laughter and love he created with his
  words
one simple thought wouldn't leave his mind
somewhere in his travels
had he made a difference
when he left this world
would he be remembered as a poem or the
  poet

Disappear

In a town filled with lights and promises
I'm the song that no one sings
Dragging my heart across broken glass
A lost jester in the rain
Just laughing through the pain

I died awhile when we first met
Silenced from the lightning strike
Then the magic happened
There's no wrong ways when it's right
Just hope filled dreams that steal the night

Take my breath
Hold my hand
Paint the sunset and sail away
To a place that feels like home
You have my heart as I'm standing here
Let our scars fall in love and disappear

Still

My mind's eye
  has seen the magic of tomorrow
How beautiful the sunrise is
  as it peels away the night
I have heard the birds
  singing on the wire
  the song of spring
  with dew fresh on the grass
I have seen your smile
  as you catch yourself daydreaming of us
How fortunate I am
  to lay my head down this night
  knowing that you'll still love me

Last Night

Last night the wind called your name and
today all I heard was your silence. How did
the moon fool me once again into believing
you'd be waiting, longing, ready to be loved.

New Beginning

In that moment
  between the darkness and the sunrise
I can smell spring trying to break free
The moisture on the grass
  mixed with the strong waft of dry Earth
  heavy under my feet
I take in the last breath of winter
  as the sun peaks its beauty over the horizon
The crisp thin air lingers in my lungs
  reminding me each dawn is a new beginning

Carry Love

As long as my heart has a beat
  it will carry your love
It has been through wars
Surrendered in defeat
Only to be set free once again
And you
  will always hold a special place inside of it
The chains you broke
  will never again keep me down
Although you may no longer hold its key
Your love will always be my strength

Sparkle

There are days when the stars line up at midnight and refuse to sparkle. Just like days when the sun calls in too gray to shine, my heart weeps at the idea of you with another. Someone less deserving. Someone that has razor blade fingers and tangled lies that are put in place to catch your breath as his forked tongue tells the stories you want to hear.

Rain Love

I want to make love to you in the rain; a summer thunderstorm, where each kiss has a purpose. I want to feel your body wrap around mine as if letting go will lose me forever. I want to feel the wind at my back as your fingers find my skin. I want to feel the rumble underneath us as the thunder rolls through our souls. I want to feel the magic of us as the lightning crashes to the ground in celebration of our love. I want to make love to you until our breath, our flesh, our bodies, become one and never again part.

Collide

As much as we want things to stay the same, they change. Time and space put wedges where every little bit of doubt lies. The heart, the mind, if you're lucky, one day they will collide.

One Day

One day
　after all the tears
I knew that every goodbye
　would be worth your hello
That every missed rose
　would somehow bloom inside your eyes
Each tear I shed
　would be wiped away
　with a simple smile across your lips
The wrong turns
I made during life's journey led me straight
　to you
Now each beat of my heart
　calls your name
　and tells me I'm home

My Beautiful

My beautiful, I have seen stars shine in your eyes. I've caught the sunrise gently cascading its kiss across your lips during the early morning hours of summer. The small of your back has been home to my hand as I slowly caressed it, falling off to sleep as if I were in a dream. I have woken to the sound of thunder, rested my ear to your chest and with each lightning strike, it was as if you were creating the symphony of hammering claps. I have watched your eyes fill with yesterday's sadness and witnessed your soul shine when love became real again. Through it all, I still look at you as if we are brand new. So please, when you lie down to rest tonight, remember me and just how pure my intentions were and still are. Wander deep inside your caged heart and find my kiss. Let it bring back the memories of the moment our lips first met and magic happened.

Salvation

I never knew unconditional love until I tasted
the broken on your lips. The way the tears
rolled off your tongue and settled into my
down-turned smile, left me longing for your
laugh. You stood watch over my hopes, held
my hand as I blew out each candle. You took
my pot of gold and turned it into a wishing
well. You became one small fix after the next
and I became the hate you had for the world.
Through it all I never prayed for salvation
until I saw the goodbye in your eyes.

Breaking Dawn

There will be days
  that the memory of my tingling touch,
  the one I offered so freely,
   will keep you from completing your easiest
  tasks
The smell of my skin
  won't allow your dawn to break
  as you toss and turn across my side of the
  bed
Reaching out your hand to hold a ghost
Getting nothing but cold sheets in return

Washed Away

Alone with her I can't help but stare
Her eyes like two beacons of light
  shining in a room full of darkness
The words I love you
  slip out like a Sunday confession
And as I await my penance
  she brings my hand to her face
Running down her cheek, under my
  fingertips
I can feel the burden she bears
Cold stinging reminders of a life left behind
I try and catch each day of her past
  in the palm of my hand
Gently brushing aside the moments
  that have stole her joy
Keeping them from hitting her quivering lips
Saving her the heartache of tasting them
  one last time

Last Call

I sit and stare at the naked trees blowing in the wind. My mind takes me back to my childhood, long before the innocence of making wishes wore thin. Now, the skeletons of the past pull up stools next to the demons of today and pass each other whiskey, while I pour your memory over melted ice and make it my last call.

Writer's Heart

If you are ever lucky enough to be in the heart of a writer, you will never die. Your story will be talked about, picked apart and lamented over for generations to come. And when the dust settles on the pages, the smiles and tears saved within will be forever remembered just as they were meant to.

Rooms

There are 'rooms' inside all of us. We create
them in our mind, our heart and our soul. We
hide there when times get too tough, when
love lets us down and when we get filled with
self-doubt. They are safe, warm and we know
that no one can hurt us there. Unfortunately,
many of us build the walls to these rooms so
high that not only do they keep anyone from
getting in, but they keep us from getting back
out. When one door closes, make sure you
don't get stuck. Don't allow yourself to dwell
in 'it' for longer than it deserves.

Beauty Hides

My heart shows the scars of all the beatings
but my soul has taken all the sorrow, all the
blessings, the lost love, the struggles, the joy
and the pain and turned me into the person I
am today and that's where the beauty hides

Battleground

Her smile
  is the beautiful place tears go to hide
They snuggle in
  nice and warm and safe
Salty to taste
  slick to the touch
Her cheeks
  have become the melting pot for joy and
  pain
Two rival gangs dancing together across her
  face
  as if they are fighting a never ending turf
  battle
The only winner is self doubt
The struggle to keep her heart beating and
  pumping love is all but lost

Wake Up

Waking up to another day is a blessing that
many take for granted. Those that have
suffered loss understand that within a
minute, a split second, the privilege can be
taken away. Stay humble my friends and
squeeze every moment out of each day.

Starshine

Somewhere in the heavens
  a star shines
The fire inside it rages
Burning bright
  with the years of lost hope
Stardust kisses fall at our feet
Reminders of the dreams we had
Your twinkling smile
  sending light our way
Please watch over us little one
In the darkest of hours
In the brightest of days
Guide us through them all

Night Demons

Sometimes I hate the night.
It's when the demons that we feared
  were under our beds all these years,
  find themselves within our minds
  and create thoughts that can only lead to
  second guessing.
But, no matter what those voices say,
 I know I love you and miss your kiss.

Tomorrow's Dream

When the hours get old
  and my life is reaching its end on this round
  rock
With nothing much more
  than the crying ahead
I will look back on my days
  with a wondrous smile
Knowing I did not walk alone
  through these extraordinary days
For I took a piece of all of you
Handshakes, laughs and dreams
Tears, hugs and memories
They will all get me through
  from this life to the next
Where ever it may be
  that my soul goes to roam
I will not tread lightly
I will not go quietly into that good night
I will leave my mark
Just as I've done here

Day 10

The sunshine and waves met at the horizon
Like two lovers endlessly searching for a
  moment alone
Each night they kissed as one faded into the
  other
Holding on for as long as possible
With the promise of waking up in each others
  arms

Whiskey Promise

Seeing her in a crowded room
Causes wonder within my head
As eyes of others watch her move
  the gestures
  the blazing stares
Those looks won't ever win her heart
If they only knew
Love doesn't come to those that beg
Our souls have fought countless wars
  to reach each other
  the bleeding
  the tears
  the 'I finally found you'
No whiskey promise will ever take that away

The Big Empty

It doesn't happen that often
  but tonight
the stars seem out of reach
Winter's cold
  has stolen the day
And this bed
  feels colder than it ever has

Too big
Too empty

Whole Again

Every now and then she gives me little pieces
  of herself
I hold them close
I cherish them
Keep them safe
So that one day
I can give them all back and make her whole
  once again

Rainbows & Lost Ships

I've seen rainbows crash in your eyes
lost ships run aground under your touch
even mountains move for you
quick to bow down to let you pass
you're an audacious force of nature
yet somehow you're afraid to leap from the
  shortest peaks
hiding inside the fear of what tomorrow will
  bring
blaming it on the fall
not knowing you will fly
and even should you crash
the universe has feathered your bed
creating a safe place to land
if only you could see
  there is no harm in the happening
that love has not found you
just to leave you abandoned once again
the fingers that hold your heart
  won't ever let it bleed
the mouth that speaks the words
  won't ever lie to your ears
they will simply kiss the smile
  that has been all but lost in a sea of tears
drowning the soul that's meant to shine

Soul Kiss

Night came and whispered your name
Left you lying there next to me
Naked and warm
The moonlight shining on your goose
  bumped skin
The ocean breeze caressing your breasts
As the sounds of crashing waves echoed
  in the distance
Your flesh jumped
  as my fingertips explored the ups and downs
Those soft places
  you only shared with a chosen few
My mouth following each curve
Until my lips
  found themselves kissing your soul

Inside

Your eyes pierce through me
  like a lightning strike
My heartbeat
  becomes a moment frozen in time
I want to see what you see
  when you look at me, as if I'm perfect
It's your hands
I want to gather the broken pieces of my past
  that you so freely let out to run wild from
  their hiding places
It's like you tend to my secret gardens
  with hope and strength
  giving me a place to call home
  inside your heart

Masterpiece

You are someone's every thought, their
scribbled lines of rhyme. You are someone's
11:11 wish and each moment of their
tomorrow with more than just ink stains on
the page. You are an unpublished
masterpiece waiting to be found.

Awake

She lies awake dreaming of a time
  when her heart didn't hurt
  and her mind didn't question
Long before
  there were scars that needed healing
She knew just what love was
Soft butterfly kisses across every inch of her
  skin
Leaping heartbeats from hearing her own
  name spoken
Dizziness from the slightest touch of his lips
And as the darkness settles into night
She lies awake dreaming
Thankful her heart took the beatings
  and her mind never stopped asking

Once Again

His eyes
  saw through the smile
His ears
  heard everything she couldn't say
He loved her
  every minute of each day since she walked
  in that door
Through the damage and destruction
  he took a place inside her heart
  long forgotten
Filling her thoughts
  more than she realized
He knew just how much she loved him
  without ever hearing a word
Yet, he could feel it coming
  the hammer would soon fall
  shattering his world into infinite pieces once
  again

Man in the Mirror

When I look in the mirror
I see a man
  that has never been good enough
It seems I'm a throw away kind of lover
The days come and go
  and so do they
My heart's scars read like a road map
  filled with detours of could have beens and
  what ifs
So beautifully painful
Like thorns on a rose
  to know love
  to feel love
  and watch it walk away

Lips

When my lips part
I like how yours fill each space between
  as if they were two puzzle pieces
that up until that moment
  never found the right fit
But most of all
I love that even in the darkest of spaces
my lips can always find yours again
whenever I need to be complete

Unanswered Prayers

Under the moon I sit
  watching the skies open
  to accept wishes of countless souls
  as they rise to the heavens
Whispers cast into the wind
  catching stars
  that shoot across the sky
Unanswered prayers
  in desperate hours
  hearts crying out
  begging not to beat alone
  and how lucky I am
  to have you
  sharing mine

Mosaic

She's like a stained glass mosaic; cracked and
  beautiful.
And I'm just the sun that gets her to shine.

Q & A

There are nights I've waited for questions
  that have never come.

But the answers have never changed...

  Yes....

  Still....

  Always....

  Yes....

That's easy, because you have filled my
heart more than anyone ever has, causing
my soul to shine and I feel incomplete
without you....

Anytime, I'm always here....

Crumbled

I caught the words
  breaking off in half silence
  as if she wanted to swallow them
  before they truly escaped her lips
  she couldn't tell me again
  and sad I was
  for not hearing it the first time
I stared in her eyes
  as they welled up with years of lost dreams
  the corner of her mouth quivered
  and her nose flared
  as if it were the dam
  that would protect her face from the flood
Without warning
  her kiss smashed my lips
  and as her tears streamed down
  I could taste her walls crumbling

Blurred Lines

Our hearts met in random rooms
Sneaking around like married lovers
  afraid to be seen together
We fooled the voices inside our heads
Kept them forever guessing
Our love lives minute by minute
Simply existing for today
But the lies we told ourselves
Became blurred lines
Between the wounds of the past
  and the hesitation of tomorrow

Sometimes

Sometimes dreams crash long before you
wake and the chance to grow old together is
burned to ashes as you're left wondering
what could have been.

When It's Over

We won't ever truly know what this life is for until it's over. But I think it's about love. It isn't fame or fortune, or material things. It's about connections and leaving a piece of yourself with everyone you meet.

At the end of it all, when I'm remembered, my only hope is that everyone will smile and offer a kind word to simply say, 'that guy wasn't an asshole.'

You're Gone

Since you're gone
There's an aching need
  to drown out the day
To wash away the taste of failing you
  that I can't seem to swallow
You are the burning shots of whiskey
  that get me through each night
The cold stinging ice water
  that awakens me each morning after

Perfection

I don't want perfection
I'd never be able to work that hard
  No
I want your scars
  so we can heal as one
Your lost days of the past
  so we can find each other tomorrow
I want to hold all the broken pieces of your
  heart
  so we know what it's like to be fully in love

When your heart beats free

Your breath shortens from just a hello

And your eyes stay wide open as you dream

Oceans

Swimming the oceans between us has left my
arms far too tired to do anything but allow
you to fall into them as they close around you

Day & Night

I miss you in the sunshine
When I can't escape the shadows
My first thought
My early morning wake up
My 12 Noon

I miss you in the darkness
When my mind is all I can hear
My last wish
My dreams at night
My 2am

Broken Glass

I was awakened before dawn
stepped out into the crisp winter air
the crunch of the frosty ground
reminded me of broken glass
and as I watched the sun rise
I couldn't help but think of you
how each day was a new beginning
how every morning brought undeniable hope
a tear ran down my cheek and met my smile
knowing for a time I held perfection in
  my hands
and that you'll live forever in my heart

Drowning

The crash was deafening
but the screams were silent
something beautiful was dying
drawing its last breath
from the wishing well
that held it captive
now it's poured out over the land
like a flood of emotion
a tidal wave of hurt and loss
drowning the soul of a lost boy

Innocent Beauty

My smile burns brightest
  when my lips say her name
it's as if the sound
  was made to roll off my tongue
bounce off the ears
  and echo through my chest
but nothing prepares me
for the innocent beauty
of when her lips speak mine

She

She's the glow of New York City lights
She's the rain on summer nights
The endless smile when I'm feeling sad

She's the late night knock at my door
She's a walk along the shore
My beating heart during a kiss goodnight

She's like snow on Christmas Eve
She's the last thing I believe
All the dreams I've ever had

She's the sun just after dawn
She's my shelter from the storm
She's every place I never want to leave

Cliches & Yesterdays

We were everything right
Just at the wrong time
All those late night promises
Of who we are and what we'd be
Are all but over now
Tiny pieces rolled up on the floor
Are all that's left of the memories I called
  home
Love is a fool's game
Living life as strangers is the reward
Cliches and yesterdays
Are what we've become
Forever only lasts as long as you let it
A soul can weep and beg and hope
But it's the heart that matters most

Each Morning Light

The sun shines through my bedroom window
Let's me know another night has passed
  without you
As I lie awake in this lonely bed
You're the only thought running through my
  head
I can still remember
How you looked the night we met
Picture perfect nervous
With a smile I can't forget
You changed my heart forever
Just by taking that first step
Though we don't see each other lately
I still love you like crazy
Had I known we would say goodbye so soon
I would have turned our pages slower
Not wishing certain days away
I should have fought harder for you to stay

Even in Paradise

I've hit walls
And they've hit back
The meaning of life and love
Isn't always plain to see
Even in paradise
The sun goes down
You lose yourself
  and a heart dies without a sound
We fight to not give in
Live life word by word
Take what we're given
  or so I've heard
We figure it out line by line
Only to be let down day by day
Just remember actions are our words
When there is nothing left to say

No Fear

If you find love in your heart, don't allow
your mind to give reasons why it won't work.
Let the heart do its job; love without fear.

When Tomorrow Comes

I went looking for proof that this isn't just a
   dream
I stare at the ceiling
My heart beating
I toss and turn trying to catch up to the plans
we made
I spend a lifetime alone without you each
   night
The mountains seem to be winning
But the struggle doesn't end
I pinch myself and feel nothing but pain
Everywhere I look I see you
But I can't get to you
Maybe that's what I'm here for
To know what dying feels like
Each and every day
Just know how hard I tried
To pick up the pieces and pave your broken
   road
I'll leave this world before I give up
So I'll be right here waiting
When tomorrow comes

Where I'll Be

When I close my eyes
You're always right here
Your skin
Tastes sweet against my lips
  as the rain falls down around us
It's just not where I'll be
I'll be finding things to pull me through
To stop my mind from thinking of you
Until the day you say hello again
But don't you worry about me coming back
Because I've never ran or left
I'm right there with you
When you close your eyes
I'm inside your every whisper goodnight
And each ray of morning sunlight

Stolen

Her mind may love the path we're on but her
heart still walks hand-in-hand with him
Her lips taste like happiness as they meet
mine but her breath cries out his name in the
  night
Her eyes show me how much she loves me
but her fallen tears have stolen the words

Stay

The heavens seem to be crying
As if something wonderful is dying
The thunder rolls
The skies tear open
Lost dreams and wasted wishes falling fast
A heart of stone finally turns to ash
Letting fate take over
Never knowing what's to come
It's all part of a bigger destiny
Just how far we'll go is up to you and I
The story gets re-written
With tears of the angels
I'd save you from this hell if I could
Just to get us back to good
How many times I've dropped to my knees
Telling myself to never let go
And on these lonely nights
I try and keep forever in my sights
The reminders of you are everywhere
But I've seen it all and should know better
Tonight I thought your love might disappear
Then I look and still find you here
Maybe because I need you but can't feel you
I don't know what to do if all I know is gone
My wings are broken like a lost blue jay
I can only beg you to please stay

Save Me

night has come and you are far away
the ticking of the clock
putting distance between us
the moon our only saving grace

do you hear my voice still whispering
  when my words are not filling your ears
  with madness

when I'm gone
do you miss my touch

does the beating of your heart
  get you to dance with the monsters inside
  your head

and as the world has you twisting around and
  around
just promise me this

somewhere between the street lights and
  stars
our scars will fall in love
  and your lips will always save me

Love Alone

I would have loved you forever
From the moment we met
Until the faded last breath
But love cannot survive on love itself
It needs to be nourished
Held tight
Kept out of harm's way
It gets darkened by minutes of betrayal
Beat down by days of loss
It tries to hang on
Until each cut goes deeper
Clinging to what it once knew
What it once was
And longs to be again
Before it was pushed to the back of the line
Before it became an afterthought
Taken for granted
Like a mindless task to fill the day
Love doesn't die alone
We kill it

Flawed Perfection

She hides her thoughts away from the world
like the shadows of the moon
but to me she's just as beautiful
in the darkness as in the light
an irreplaceable gift
that day by day becomes unwrapped
to show more of her flawed perfection

The Way You Shine

The lights of this town
  can't hold a candle to the way you shine
  like a shooting star
  across the midnight sky
  full of magic and mystery
You're like
  a thousand little lightning strikes
  electrifying my senses
Crashing into me
  burning through my skin
  straight to my beating heart

Imperfect

Embrace your flaws.
You may be weathered and worn
  tattered and torn
  battered and bruised
  but you are not broken
Know that you've become perfectly imperfect

The Darkness

I will follow you into the darkness
The ever changing chaos of your mind
And be there when the screams come
To offer the silence of my sanity
So that you one day can smile
Knowing you are never alone

Rain Dance

I want to dance with you in the rain
  and the darkness
Inside the perfect storm
The wind whipping at our backs
Our lips barely close enough to touch
Our skin soaking wet
It's as close to making love to you
  as I can be
Without going insane and losing my mind

Love Tales

When we read tales of love
It's stories of Heaven
Magical lightning crashes
And happily ever after
But when I think of love
I picture a friendship set on fire
Two souls willing to take a chance
And the stars granting the heart one wish

Beginning of the End

There were moments
When my beginning was your end
My heart was your beat
Your smile met mine and our souls touched
It was at those times
I was the most scared I've ever been in all my
  days
I trembled with every kiss
Scared of how high I felt
Afraid of how far I'd fall if you ever left

Forever

Did you ever think the person you'd meet,
would be someone you knew forever? Like a
rain drop lost in a river. A snowflake blown
by the wind. The hand of fate plucked you
from the heavens and sent you straight to
me.

Demons

I've outlived all my demons
Silenced every ghost
Walked these halls
and left the past behind
Mirrors filled with memories
No longer holding me to the life I used to
  know

Heavens

Leave the splintered pieces
They'll pick themselves up
They always do
The moon will shine on another night
Stars will shoot more empty wishes across
  the sky
And the Heavens will close the book on you
  and I

Her Moonlight

Do you see that moonlight?
It shines just for her
On dreams that passed her by
On places she's never seen
On a smile that once gave life
But was lost somewhere in between
  the lies and promises
Hanging there waiting for someone
  to prove her wrong
That love's not a fool's game
That every man isn't the same
That when it's all been said and done
She wouldn't have simply loved and lost
But she loved and loved and lost and lost
  and then she was found
Do you see that moonlight?
It shines just for her
So she can be found

Dream Another Day

As I look past the calm river
On this beautiful sunny day
I am lost in thought
Accompanied only by your smile
At home inside your deep dark eyes
I breathe you in
Not wanting to let the moment end
I hold my breath
And can feel your heart beat with mine
Your skin feels like silk
As your arms wrap around me
Keeping me safe from harm
The cool breeze blows
Your long hair covers us
Blocking this world away
I can taste your lips
As I whisper 'I am yours'

And you are gone
Leaving me to dream another day

Beautiful Disaster

Looking over the edge of forever
Tied to a lover's cross
Only to be cut down
          into
          the
          bottomless
          void
          of
          self
          doubt
Sacrifice the heart
Just to save the soul
Your eyes always told me
'I cannot stay'
Like a beautiful disaster
The memories will last a lifetime
Burned deep into my mind's eye
Every stolen breath
Every sweet lipped kiss
Every word you could not say

Through It All

Dreaming wide awake
I'm seeing things for the first time
After endless tears and loss
I've learned to laugh and love
Some days I wander through this maze
And when there's no way out
You're the sunshine through the haze
Let your heart beat free
Even during the darkest days
This world spins me around
Puts me where I need to be
In a place where your lips hold my very last
  breath
Where your eyes are the only light I see
The deeper I get
The harder I fall
I'm right there with you
Through it all

By Your Side

Though they were few
the nights falling asleep with you by my side
will forever be cherished moments of my life
In the morning
I would wake just to watch you breathe
During the night
I would touch you so I knew I wasn't
  dreaming
It was at those times
when I knew happiness was not what you get
  but what you give
I was as close to heaven as a breathing being
  can be
When I was by your side

Echoes

I will always remember your soft whispers in
that crowded room, as you leaned in to tell
me you loved me. How each word stung my
ears and made them ring. If those were the
last words I ever heard, the echoes would last
a lifetime.

These Words

These words
What do I do with them
They slip to the tip of my tongue
Only to be choked down
Like a twisted rusty sword
They stay lodged inside my throat
Never being set free
Swallow them down
And make a wish
That one day you'll hear me

These words
Get left unsaid
With each day that passes
Slip through lost moments of time
Scattered across our lives
They could fill a book of a thousand pages
Each one written the same
Your ears never hearing
What my lips long to say
And alone I cry your name

These words
Can say so much
Brighten your darkest paths when heard
And cripple your faith when they aren't

Three little words
Bigger than life itself
That get taken for granted by countless
  hearts

Over and over and again
Said to those that don't deserve
But I knew them right from the start

Open Letter To My 15 year Old Self

I saw him again today, that boy I used to be. Remembering my first heartbreak, sitting alone on the back steps after school. I spoke to him as if I had gone back in time, knowing what I know today. I told him that she was a lesson and there would be more to come. Each one teaching him something new, but none would hold him for too long. I explained how none of them would cherish the love he gave. Until one day he'd be found by the most beautiful and complicated soul to ever grace this world. She will make him forget everything he once thought of love because she will teach him about life and that true love is just as much about someone else's happiness as it is his own. Deep love that only two lost souls can make sense of. Don't let her go, I told him. Fight every day to keep her. Make her smile and though she won't ever believe you, tell her just how beautiful she really is. Fill each of her days with love and laughter and never take one single moment with her for granted. I assured him on the day that angel clips her wings for him, all the pieces of his past will fall together and he'll know why it never was meant to be with anyone else.

The Next Step

Our journeys change once we find the
  destination
One day we'll look back on these moments
  able to retrace our footsteps
  and see just how we got here
The broken roads
The less traveled paths
The twists and turns
Those moments we walked alone
  in search of our second half
And days our paths crashed into one another
Forever changing how we choose the next
 step

Silent Desire

There are corners of our mind
Where all of our thoughts go to hide
The bits and pieces of our past
Sit and stain our memories
The doubts and wishes of tomorrow
Bring about an anxious uncertainty
My silent desire for you
Makes its home there
Between the words that are left unspoken
And those that I scream from rooftops
Hoping that you'll hear me

Scars & Rainbows

She thanked each rainbow that never
   brought gold
Smiled at every dark cloud that shaded her
   days
And kissed each scar on her broken heart,
   the day he walked into her life

Wide Eyes

It's not that you drive me crazy
I was there long before I met you
You take me to a place that reminds me of
   what it was like to be a child
With wide eyes and wishes
Long before I doubted myself and every
choice I made
I want you to know, you were my greatest
decision
And as time goes by, I see more of your flaws
You allow me in to more of the dark spaces
   that have kept you shaking for so long
   and I love you more and more each day

Because Forever

Promise me if I stay
The darkness we share
  will always be filled with your light
That our lips will never lie
And we'll find the truth
  in every stolen kiss
Our good nights
Will never be goodbye
Because forever
  is far too long to go without you

Inside Her Heart

His eyes saw through the smiles
His ears heard everything she couldn't say
He loved her, every minute of each day since
  she walked in that door.
He took a place inside her heart long
  forgotten
And filled her thoughts more than she
  realized
He knew just how much she loved him
  without ever hearing the words

Crash

Their skin crashed like a violent ocean wave when it meets the sand. Each one taking a piece of the other. The sting brought back memories of when she felt alive. Now her burning soul ached from within and it was his mouth and hands that lit the flame.

Heart of a Woman

There is no better place to be than secure in the heart of a woman. A good man won't ever break it and a better man will remind her that she has one that's still whole and very capable of love.

Last Breath

Promise me that if you should ever tire of me, your lips will not deceive me, that your voice will whisper to me in the wind and I will suck your breath in one last time so I won't drown in my sea of tears

The Storm

It's as if the storm has been raging
  since I don't know when
Tossing tears around like waves
Beating the heart inside my chest
  into submission
If I could abandon my mind
Leave it alone somewhere else
Then maybe the dark cloud would lift
Please leave the light on
  during the darkness
One day I'll return
Weathered but ready
For my soul will always be half yours.

Lost Souls

I want you to come down from the heavens,
or up from the Earth and grant me my wish

Make the world go away and just leave the
lost souls so that we may finally find one
another

What If

The universe, with all its elements and wonders, can sometimes leave you feeling baffled at its achievements. Of all the twists and turns we take, how is it that we still fight it, make excuses for and fail to see, that paths collide when they are meant to. Some say it's a predestined future. Others say it's fate or things simply happen without reason. But then tell me why the moment I saw you, my heart leaped out of my chest. Tell me why my mind races each day to find the words to say. Why my soul aches every minute when you're away. They say we have a soul mate, a second half of ourselves to make us whole. If that is true, then you are mine. Your cautious feet, balance my flight fancy wings. Your distance, makes up for my desire to fill every inch between us with laughter and love. Your way of living life under the veil of 'what if', hides my need to die in your arms every night.

Her Gift

If I could own the moon, I'd give you the side
that shines to light up your life during its
darkest hours

Stars

It's not the letting go
it's the watching you walk away
while I sit here
under a sky filled with your dreams
dreams we shared with one another
dreams you made
when you thought no one was listening
they all hang there together
without a place to land
without a soul to save

Become One

Live this dream
as it breaks through the darkness
just waiting for the light of day

Lift it to the heavens
where it will be safe
from the river of emotions
that run through your veins

Take my heart
hold it within your deepest depths
together we can jump off this mountain
that's in our way

Lay down beside me
allow your most precious fears
to break the fall

Kiss me
let your darkest desires
part my lips and dance across my tongue
so I can taste your passion
as we become one

The Thorns

Midnight sun breaks through the night
Your beautiful face my only sight
Our nights together
  living apart
So much to say
  but where to start

Every time I've lived with love
Seems I touch each thorn along the rose
Can I pick myself up off the floor
Walk away from the open door

The lights go out
  the day it ends
My mind races and this whole world spins
Holding onto dreams
  facing days alone
Counting each hour until I'm home

Autumn

She was as fragile as an autumn leaf
restlessly shaking
as the winds of change swept through
clinging to all she knew
afraid to fall
not knowing where she'd land
but just as each leaf does
she finally let go and found she could fly
and even if for just a little while
she felt alive and beautiful

Irreplaceable

My heart breaks
  for those that lose faith in love
Those that are hurt and never heal
The heart is made to take a beating
Know that with each lost love
  comes wisdom and knowledge
  of what you don't want
Be thankful for those that left
It frees up the space needed
  for the one that finds you irreplaceable

Where You'll Be

Seems half my life I've been searching
Standing out in the pouring rain
Faking smiles I did my best
Just to hide away the pain
I never knew there were angels
Until you walked through that door

Since you're gone
I only long for more
I want to run to you
Let you know tomorrow will be OK
I need to see your face
Tell you all the words I couldn't say

The good times shared together
Are all that I remember

Stolen kisses at midnight
The summer moonlight shining in your hair
When I close my eyes at night
You are still right there
Waiting for me in my dreams
Close enough for me to touch or so it seems

And that's just where you'll be tonight
When I lay my head down and say goodnight

A Day Away

Love is never lost
Especially after I found you
The nights still seem long
But the days keep me strong
Because tomorrow is just a day away

There never is enough time
Forever can barely hold it
All the love I have for you
I share with smiles and sometimes tears
And tomorrow is just a day away

I wake up to the hope of you
I end my nights wishing
Knowing that it's all I've got
Until tomorrow

But tomorrow is just a day away

As If

I fell IN
You pushed me OUT
I let you GO
As IF
the CHOICE were mine to make
As IF
I had control of

the WHEN
          [seconds after you said goodbye]
the WHERE
          [sitting alone with my regrets]
the HOW
          [into a million pieces]
My HEART would break

Crumble

Share with me your worries
unleash all your demons on me
  and we
will fight this world together
until each wall
crumbles to the sea

Clear Skies

The river of tears I had cried carried me to where I needed to be. Its surface, like mirrored glass, stared back at me. I was alone and safe, surrounded by mountains of hope and beautiful clear skies. I knew I had made it through the darkest days of my past and each bright tomorrow was carved out ahead of me.

Promises

Promises that aren't meant to be kept, will criss-cross your heart with scars and taint the view through rose colored glasses. Every tear that ever formed at her feet was put there by someone who found her disposable. If she only knew that love was hers for the taking. Glory days of life, laughter and loyalty. A golden heart that would break down the walls she built only to build them back with wide open windows and him inside.

A Cold December

I thought of you today as a cloud passed over head and a rain drop hit my face. I pictured your lips kissing my cheek and I was lost. For a moment I was standing outside on a cold December night. It was the first time my lips tasted yours. How I wished time would stand still. I wanted that magic to last forever. It felt as if I had been struck by lightning; quick and beautiful. A memory I'll never forget.

Sunset

Sometimes the answers never come
For those times
I wish I had one more day with you
So if tomorrow should never come
  and
My heart can longer hold a beat
Remember me in your sunset sky
I'll be
That last twinkle of light
Just before the night

The Last Goodbye

With that first hello
You found me
Standing here alone
In the ashes of lost love
Thinking hope was almost gone

I wonder if you see me
As the simple man I am
Filled with dreams and passion
Trying to make my life much better
Not wasting it on days gone by

I wonder if you feel me
As night turns to day and back again
Reaching for you as I dream
I'm lost and far from home
And it's you I need to hold

I wonder if you hear me
With so much yet to say
My mouth moves but there's no sound
Calling your name in silence
Waiting for the last goodbye

Love Moments

He loved her. Not the type of love you share between friends and family. No, this love couldn't be spoken. There were not enough words to carry it all. She was his answer to every question why and from time to time, her mind allowed her heart to beat free. He promised to always be there for each one of those moments.

Summer Dream

It had been weeks, months, since he had seen her. Never gone from his thoughts, always longing to hold her in his arms once again. And on a cool summer night, as the moon chased one day into the next, he found his home. With just one kiss, he returned to every smile she put across his face and every vision of heaven his mind had ever dreamed.

Fool's Paradise

I could feel the air escape my lungs as if it were a dying breath. The tears wouldn't come. They were frozen, lost within eyes that have been blessed with seeing the beauty of you; both inside and out. Alone I sit holding onto a broken soul that won't allow itself to believe, that the second half of it had been found, then torn away, to never be reunited. Had my words lit up your smile for the last time? Were our tomorrows meant to be set adrift, abandoned and never be thought of again? Each day without you finds me clawing at the chains that keep our hearts from beating as one. Every step that takes me away from you, leaves my bones broken and bent. I scream in silence in this boundless cage of a fool's paradise.

Something Beautiful

The doors were left opened. The past stretched out as far as the eye could see. The future, although bright, was hidden behind the walls built to keep from ever being blind sided. Today it's time to let go. Lock those doors. Throw away the key and head out to find something beautiful.

River Rain

Raindrops hit the river
  like a million razor blades
Piercing its surface
  as if trying to wash itself new again
The sun breaks from the clouds
Shining a rainbow of hope
  onto the face of a tired soul
blazing a trail
  to a pot of gold filled with broken dreams
  and stolen wishes
until this day had all but been forgotten
Tossed aside like yesterday
Rummage through the heap and make
yourself new again
Clean the slate
Follow that rainbow back to a day
  when dreams were everything you held onto
  and magic was at your fingertips

Beat of My Heart

I have stared into those beautiful eyes
Kissed your lips goodnight
And drifted off to sleep a thousand times
You're my first thought as the sun rises
My last thought when it sets
The hours I spend without you
Seem to last a hundred days
What started out as a lump in my throat
Has become the beat of my heart

Break Free

Each line upon her face had its own story.
Every scar across her heart made it harder
for her to accept true love. And all her tears,
one-by-one, took a little piece of her back to
the sea, creating waves that crashed against
the shore like fists beating down the walls
that held her captive, never allowing her past
to ever break free.

Shine On Me

I thought love had come and gone
Leaving me lost like an abandoned soul
Hurt always took the place of happiness
But here you are, deep inside my heart
Where I've built up walls to keep love out
My eyes always hiding the fears of letting go
  again
Tomorrow may still be lost in the shadows
Hidden from our view
Never revealing its fate
But the bricks have crumbled
Piece by piece they'd been chipped away
Without knowing it, you have done the
  impossible
Breaking the chains holding me down
Your smile is like a brand new dawn
Shining on me
Guiding me through the dark
Leading me out of this scar filled maze

Fairy Tale Life

My life has never been about the fairy tale. I don't want to find a sleeping beauty in the woods or a woman who can't keep her shoes on during her only night off. No, I want someone as real as life itself. Someone that has gotten up one more time than she's been knocked down. A woman that knows her worth, who is comfortable in a five-star restaurant but isn't afraid to wear sweat pants and a t-shirt, with no make-up, while eating pizza on the couch watching the game. I want someone as broken and bent as I am. Someone who has parts of her that are tarnished but still isn't afraid to let the light fill every crack of all the scars that were left by those things that didn't kill her. I want the woman that still believes in true love. I want someone to dance in the rain with and though I know there's not a pot of gold waiting at the end of any rainbow, I want to find heaven in every skipped through puddle. Now that I think of it, maybe it is a fairy tale.

Caged Heart

here we are face to face
staring down the demons
screaming in the night
second chances come to those that wait
lost souls and gypsy hearts on the mend
love can be bitter sweet
lose a piece of you
to make room for the other
if my words alone could break down the walls
I'd speak them constantly
throw them like hammers
until each block crumbled to ashes
and every scar was healed smooth
allowing your caged heart to beat free again

Never Forget

Never forget
Those moments when you were mine
Please take my heart
Keep it close
  and I'll never be too far
Here I am tonight
Feeling like I'm your last thought
That your hello is really goodbye
My heart aches
Each time the phone rings
  and you're not there
Each morning comes
  and I fall apart all over again
I lost you once
  and now I just can't let you go

Second Chance

There are doors that open allowing us peeks
at the past. Brilliant reminders of what could
have been. Every now and then our travels
take us over the same stretch of road
along our journey. It's at those points when
the universe offers a second chance and it's
our responsibility to take it or let it pass by.

Moonbeams

Between the raindrops
  and the moonbeams
I sometimes see you staring at me
  as if I'm a mystery
Like you're a young girl again
  with the world still left to discover
Where everything was still beautiful
  and nothing hurt
At that moment
I get lost in those baby brown eyes
and you are gone again

Smiles Touch

I asked her what she liked most about being
with me. Her response was simple, she said, 'I
love when our smiles touch and I can feel our
souls dancing with each other.'

You

You are my beginning
The first ray of light
To brighten my morning
The fresh start to each amazing day
That unfolds before me

You are my west my east
My north and south
No matter where these roads take me
I am safe because you are by my side

You are my end
The moon glow
That guards each dream at night
When I lay my head to rest
You're the only wish I need granted

You are my joy
My heartbeat
My last breath
You are the better half of me

Let It Be

After all the sorrow
After all the pain
I knew there would be sunshine
A beautiful day after the rain
Just one look in your eyes and I knew
the missing piece of life was you
The road we've walked to get here
May have been long and filled with tears
We've finally found our way
Ready to cherish each and every day
Take my hand and let's just see
Where life can lead
Let's skip through the puddles
Dance in the rain
Laugh with me
Love with me
And let what will be...be

Chances Are

Chances are that the sun will rise
  tomorrow
    the next day
      even behind gray skies

Your smile may have lit my world
  tonight
    yesterday
      for the last time

And our story will never be told
  the smiles
    the tears
      how we grew old

Home

The night is always the hardest
Shooting stars stealing wishes
As the midnight sun shines
It's when you're furthest away
But closest to my heart
Holding onto a dream
Being apart with just a memory
Taking the path less traveled by
To pave this broken road smooth
It's your song that makes me sing
And your smile that takes me home

Never Goodbye

I can still feel your lips on mine
As I watch you walk away
It's what's the hardest
They say that love is blind
But I can see the sadness in your eyes
Knowing it's not what you want
Feeling torn inside to stay
When you're hurting inside so am I
I have daydreams of morning kisses and
  midnight bliss
Tonight as you try and rest
I hope your heart hears this

  Goodnight my love
    Never goodbye

Right Here

You are what I'd see
If angels had a face
When your nights are too long
Your days have been too strong
My heart will be the place
When it's love you need
Unconditionally
True
And it won't ever run
My heart has taken all the beatings
Broken and battered
The scars are reminders of what I fight for
Endless tomorrows holding you
And all my dreams coming true in your eyes
How I wish to see the morning sun cast across
  your lips
The same lips
  that have taken my breath away a thousand
  times
I am right here waiting for you
So where do we go from here
You hold the key to the next open door

My Light

You're the light I see
You brighten even the darkest days of me
I'd been searching everywhere
Before I saw you waiting there
When I looked into your eyes
I found myself again
Sometimes I come undone
Wondering if I missed the one

Paint the sunset and slip away
Lay down beside me
Wake up in my arms
And live our dreams together
When my eyes can't see you
Let me know you're with me
On these cold and lonely nights
You'll always be my light

Till the End

If only dreams could bring you back
I'd meet you in my memories
Then next to me is where you'd be
I didn't know we'd only get one chance
That our time would fly by so fast
You're the one thing I'll always need
If only there was a way we could rewind
Take our time and redefine
Make each day a new beginning
We'd see just how long love could last
I worry that I've lit up your eyes
  for the last time
Seems I'm always just that step behind
Did you stop wishing on it
Give up waiting for it
With each night that comes then goes
I wonder if I'm on your mind
With all the time that's passed
I still feel brand new from your 'hellos'
Did you hear my whisper
The night we said goodbye
Saying that the missing piece to me was you
Wishing you had stopped and turned around
These are the words you would have heard
  'I'll wait for you forever
  You'll never be alone
  Because I'll love you till the end'

How It Goes

Tonight the light seems like it's the darkest
The tears of my past taste bitter still
Open the door for another day
Take the next step and I'll be on my way

Days and nights go by and by
Leaving regrets and smiles the same
Wishing upon shooting stars
Hoping to be lying right where you are

Struggles, hard times and sleepless nights
No tea leaves or a crystal ball
Just a heart on my sleeve
Wishing to wake up tomorrow and still
  believe

I can't say what the future brings
I'm sure there are hellos and goodbyes I
  haven't heard
This is my story and how it goes
  and so will you soon I suppose

Love & Daylight

One the days when you're not strong
Never feel you're weak
It's at that time
When things are at their darkest
The love of another will give you strength
To break down your walls

When you don't feel worthy of it
Love will always find a way
While you're walking through hell
You'll find heaven
It will keep you safe from harm
Carry you high and get you home

During the nights that you're not brave
Never live in fear
Hidden in all the darkness
You will find the light
Loving someone freely will give you the
    courage
To find that tomorrow is a brighter day

I know that I could love you
There are days I already have
You take away the pain
During the nights that I'm insane
In love and daylight
Is where I see myself with you

Walking Away

Walking away isn't the hardest part. It's the mornings I wake up and reach out my hand, touching a cold sheet where your body used to lie. The minutes during lunch hour usually shared with you, even if they were texts on a screen, are now spent wondering whose words are filling your fingers. It's the hour before bedtime, when our days were shared and we were the only two people in the world. As I lay here, dreaming wide awake, I can feel your lips on mine and I wonder who is kissing you now.

Star Staring

I was staring at the stars, wondering which one held your wish, so that I could pluck it from the sky and carry it around in my pocket until I could make it come true, when I stumbled and fell, losing my count and leaving me guessing. But as I sit here waiting for the sun to visit the other side of the world once again, know that your laughter gives way to my smile. Your eyes let me see all my tomorrows laid out in front of me and your kiss fills me with life that I cannot wait to live.

Street Lights & Stars

I sit and stare at the clock
Watching the hands
 wrap themselves around the hours
the seconds ticking
 like the heart in my chest
echoing loudly inside the hole
 left when you said goodbye
I wonder what thoughts fill your mind
 am I a forgotten memory
a secret to never be spoken again
or is my name at the tip of your tongue
ready to escape your lips
just as yours is whispered
 each night from mine
and somewhere between the street lights and
 stars I hope you hear me

Absolute Beauty

She was the sight of beauty
 that I always imagined I'd see
Although she had scars
 she hid them well
When she allowed me to peel back her layers
 I could see them
and they made her absolutely beautiful

Shine

I guess you didn't understand
Maybe you didn't want to
Love doesn't die
There will always be a piece of you
  within me
I carry it
Looking back at it often
  with tears at times
  but mostly smiles
No matter how short the shine
You were my light
You showed me love
We created magic
That can never be lost
Our words
  will be remembered
Our hearts
  will always hold each others beat

Make Believe

I wake up all alone
I've lost you to the night
Reaching out but you are gone
Left wishing for the morning light

The clock on the wall freezes
Thought after thought running free
In my world full of make believe
Your smile is all I see

I sit and stare in darkness
Your face is on my mind
Minutes turn to hours
Searching for the words to find

I lie awake in silence
Thinking of days gone by
They don't have a rhyme or reason
Or answer the question why

When tomorrow comes
And the sun washes away the moon
I'll hold on to knowing
You'll be in my dreams soon

The Flame

Your hands hold my heart
it's yours to break
should you so choose
but somehow I know it's safe
lying in your fingers
wrapped gently in your grasp
letting it beat along with yours
as if we were one from the beginning
two souls connected
through time
  and space
    and wishes
      and wants
How I thought our hours had passed
fleeting visions of a lover's crush
gone but not forgotten
with one smile across the room
we found it
the spark that lit the flame
that had always been ready to burn

One Mistake

I look deep into your eyes
Pain is what I see
I wish I could take away the confusion
Put there because of me
Misunderstood moments
Can cause a heart to ache
Don't let it end
All for one mistake
The walls may seem closer
The past rushing back like a dream
Your smile is what you show
When inside you want to scream
The soft place you found
Will always be right here
Allow the love back in
To take away your fear

Wrong Love

Love has no guarantees. Countless souls have
experienced the right love at the wrong time.
It doesn't mean it's not true, only that your
lives have not aligned. Don't love with
conditions or the belief that it will be
returned. True love is about someone else's
happiness as much as your own.

Write Her

She asked me to write a poem for her, but if she only knew, she was already each word I spoke and every song I sang. She's my 'good morning world' and my 'goodnight moon'. Her smile is what I hang my dreams on at night and her eyes hold each sunrise I ever hope to see.

Blind Faith

The hours feel like weeks
The morning bleeds into night
You're right there with me
  trying to keep it all in sight
Will you promise me
We just won't throw it all away
Hold onto dreams
Always remember the words we say
I don't know what the next day will bring
Just how I feel today
I wish I had your smile to soothe me
To take some of the pain away
Running on blind faith
Knowing this is right
I close my eyes to end this day
Bringing dreams of you to me tonight

Without Words

I find myself in your eyes
Living day to day
Opening doors
Choosing paths
Never to be lost again
Losing fear
Gaining strength
Learning dreams do come true
Turning stones
Making wishes
Through the good
Through the bad
Without words
Your smile saves me
From a past with some regrets
Leading me to a lifetime
Experiencing the best

One Last Try

What if our love is lost behind a faded
  promise
Made when your heart belonged to another
Could I take you away
Go as far as fear allows
Only to find ourselves beside each other
Where love and hope collide
My whole life has had you in it
Sorry it took until now to find you
I hope it's not too late
For one last try
To show you that love's not always the same
You were born to be cherished
Shown love by more than words
Protected from all you fear inside
When you feel weak
I'll be your strength
Your soft place to land when the ride is too
  hard
Love knows no time
It knows no circumstance
Just when it's true
And that's why I love you
I'll never be your first
We both have come too far for that
But maybe with Heaven's grace
I can be your last

Not This Time

Our days were written in the stars
But today
I just need time
Time I don't want to lose
Because losing you is not the answer
But today
It seems darker than ever
Without you here with me
I mumble and scream
Things I need to say
But today
Keeps moving on
Through the dust and dark
And the cold nights where love is hard to find
Because today
I'm missing you again
Guess some memories will have to get me
    through
Instead of holding you when I'm just too far
    away

My Way

I think this whole world's gone crazy
No one makes it out alive
Fight through every hurdle
Do what you need to just survive
You find a heart to hold
Keep it close and don't let go
Say the words you need to say
And always let that person know;
I've cherished each smile you ever gave me
even during your darkest days
You're the angel that was sent here to save
  me
Always thankful you looked my way

Little Things

Love doesn't ask for much
Just a passing smile or a gentle touch
It could be a soft kiss good morning
Or a long kiss goodnight
Maybe it's a walk in the rain
Hand in hand on the beach
A pair of red roses
Mixed with carnations in bloom
Godiva chocolates and butterfly kisses
How about a couple of each
It could be an encouraging word
  in the moments we're weak
It's all the little things
Our hearts long for and seek

Yours

You shook me to me knees
I had survived letting the walls crumble
Yet my heart was still whole
Full of scars
But one just the same
Like a thief in the night
You stole all I knew of self preservation
With just one kiss
One that left our lips numb
Not a short quick kiss
But one with meaning
Pressing your mouth hard against mine
As if your soul were trying to speak to me
The darkness filled with light
And from that moment forward
It didn't matter if I was lost
You had found me
 I was yours

Butterfly Kisses & Handshakes

I wish I was still a child
Playing out in the rain
For hours of endless fun
Instead of washing away the pain
The street lights were the end of your day
Not an empty bed
Or thoughts running through your head
Wish I didn't know now
What I didn't know then
Youth is wasted on the the young
But they're spared reality

Sometimes I wonder
If this is as good as it gets
The roller coaster of ups and downs
Life was simple when ice cream was your only
  thought
Your friends were forever and love was
  butterfly kisses and handshakes

Silence

She let her eyes fall away from his stare
  long enough to take a deep breath
She caught her courage before it escaped
  through the pores of her skin again
She could feel the words starting to form
her mouth made the movement
  but the words were silent
She lifted her head higher towards the sun
Her mouth trying again to form the words
  she had been needing to say
But again she spoke in silence
She had wasted too many years with broken
  love
Never knowing what to do
  when one so true found its way in
Her mind held her heart captive
She had hesitated
Her own soul had betrayed her
Now the moment was gone
So was he

The Dance

Strength is how we measure
  how well we hide the pain
Rainbows are simple reminders
  we made it through the rain
Even during the darkest times
  there's blue skies behind the gray
If you can make it through the night
  you'll find a brighter day
Living life is a twist of fate
Nothings guaranteed
  but still worth the chance
Loving - learning
  just enjoying the dance

The Pieces

You're like sugar and razor blades
Tear filled smiles
Ghosts that haunt me on my best day
But if you were to be gone from my life
  it would tear me apart
I hold our memories close
Hoped to hold you closer
I can't stop the rain
Can't take away all the pain
No sunshine after midnight
Just a promise of starting new
Holding onto something
Not wanting to watch it lose its light
Burning down walls
Only to see them built higher once again
Let me go
Tell me goodbye
Make these dreams stop trying to die
Sail away to our paradise island
Rescue me from what's inside
Bright lights and frowning smiles
All too familiar these days
I'm left picking up the pieces
Don't love me for what I'm not
Don't lie to me for what I am
Your biggest mistake
Your most precious gift
The soft place to land in a hardened world

Shattered

Her tears landed on the windows of my mind
  shattering them
  into a millions pieces
  that threw my thoughts
  in a million directions
leaving me lost and not wanting to be found
  hurt and humbled
  cherishing my humanity
understanding that love does not guarantee
  forever
you'd be lucky if love guarantees today
the broken being I had become was all but
  hollow
 The bandages covered long standing scars
  from the thorns of roses
  that grabbed my skin
   pulling at every inch
trying to break through the cage
  to stab my steel heart
the memories remain
  from a time
when butterfly kisses and handshakes meant
 something
  but now
   whispers
    lies
     and back alley promises
      steal the show
the same walls I built to keep others out
are the same walls that keep me in

never experiencing life how it's supposed to
be lived
  a crumbled soul lies in waiting
for a day when the sun wont cast a shadow
  on the faults and failures
that have kept me stumbling on from day to
day
grasping at straws
  trying to hold on to yesterdays
  and harness the wind
    that steals dreams
    and hurls wishes into space
leaving tomorrow just out of reach
  alone and broken
    Shattered in a million pieces

Leap

The mind is the keeper of the heart
A stonewall built to protect it from dying

What the mind doesn't know
  is if the heart isn't leaping
  it's not living

Climb to the highest mountain
Scream to the heavens
Hold hands and let go
Soar above all that you fear
letting blind faith guide your way
Love's beauty is in the bloom
and just before you crash
a magical mystery will break your fall

Paths Collide

This rain comes pouring down
Like tears straight from heaven
The keeper of the stars had a plan
Our paths crossed
When they were meant to be
Now when I close my eyes
You're all I see
Leaves hit the ground
In a chilly morning breeze
Rolling around together
Like the memories I hold of a time
   when we both could smile
Now I keep them close
Waiting for the day
We both can breathe as one again
For the first time in life
I'm scared of what tomorrow brings
Not holding any control
Never seeing what's in front of me
Just what I want it to be
I stare out my window
As I lay my head to rest
Gaining comfort knowing that we share the
   same sky
There's things I don't understand
Questions that have no answers
And some I may never know the reason why
I make a wish on a falling star
Hoping we have a chance
To roll the dice one more time

Walk side by side

And let our paths collide

Here I Am

Your eyes cut through me
  like a knife through ice
peeling back the layers to reveal what I am
  made of
What sins and tragedies have built me
How far I have come
How deep my love goes
How high the walls have been built

Here I am for you to see
Open
Vulnerable
Showing the pieces of me
  that only a few have seen

It may all seem so complicated
Your love
My love
Everything in the way
It really is so simple
You're the sun behind my gray skies
and I am your rainbow after the rain

Nothing

She smiles as she tells me
                "NOTHING"

But what lives behind this 7 letters is
                "EVERYTHING"

She smiles that beautiful smile as she tells me
                "NOTHING"

In silence I gaze into her eyes and say
                "ME TOO"

Play It Again

My guitar lies bleeding, crying just for you
My heart's beat keeps the rhythm
  as my tears strum the tune
Our memories and dreams the chorus
and your name my favorite verse

From a Distance

From a distance
these words
look like a series of jumbled letters
tossed across a page
but please look closer
they have a life of their own
a heartbeat that rises and falls
they are pieces of the past
a quick glimpse into the deepest spaces
  within me
Fears
Love
Hope
Loss
Joy
Sadness
Each one pulled from a memory or created by
  desire
these words may not be much
but please look closer
they found their way from their own guarded
  rooms
to the tips of my fingers for you
these words may be all you see
but please look closer
with each line written
with each letter placed
I reveal a little more of me
I journey down
into the places where all my demons have
  been hiding

standing there facing the beast once again
praying I don't fall back in
afraid of never getting out

From a distance
these words
look like a series of jumbled letters
tossed across a page
but please look closer
because these words are made up of me

The Destination

Her hands grabbed my own
Both of hers barely able to hold one of mine
She held onto it as if it were the net that
  would save her
From the daily trapeze act that she dared to
  pull off
Without any 'ooohs' and 'aaahs'
No roar of the crowd but done just the same

Her mind had become one 'what if' thought
  after the next
A constant desire to turn the pages of her
  life's own tale
To see if the slipper finally fit
To find out if every coin flipped into
  countless fountains
Would pave her way to happily every after
Or were they simply deals made with the
  devil
On her way to the middle

Behind the sadness of her eyelids
She had seen far too many years of heartache
She stared into my eyes
As if she were reading every page of my past
Each 'wish you were here' postcard I never
  sent
Every smile I ever faked
When my life passed out lemons instead of
  nectar
It felt as if she was always there

Through the trials and tribulations
Crying through the laughter
Smiling through the pain
On my road to nowhere

And as I caught the tear of happiness running
  down her face
The bitter years she left behind
Tasted sweet against my lips
I knew she wasn't part of the journey
She was the destination

Crystal Ball

I'm a man of limited vocabulary
I lost the need for bullshit long ago
Say what you mean and do what you say
Don't disguise your intentions with
   innuendos
Life isn't lived in a crystal ball and
I'm no mind reader

Heart and Mind

We walk this journey, each day allowing the
struggle between the head and chest to
dictate our next move. Keeping us forever
locked inside the rooms we create for
ourselves that no one can enter with the key
we buried so long ago. When your mind and
heart hope and hurt for the same person,
don't ever let them go.

A Little Jay on Jay

I am a New York based writer and poet. I grew up in the awe inspiring Hudson Valley area, 60 miles from the greatest city in the world and smack dab in the middle of tranquility and grace. I have had a passion for writing since I was a small child. Being near the Hudson River and water has always helped me find my voice. I find clarity there and a simple no cost way to re-align when things get a bit askew.

Since I can remember, I have loved to write and tell stories. There has always been something special about pen and paper. As a child I remember sitting next to my mother with a yellow legal pad and black felt pen mimicking her cursive writing. Even today I prefer writing by hand to electronic means. I keep a spiral notebook in each room for anytime an idea may arise.

My love for words started when I discovered music. As a teenager anytime I'd get a new album, I'd immediately open up the lyric sheet to read the words even before I listened to the song. As you read in the introduction, my love of poetry began after reading Robert Frost's 'The Road Not Taken' in my college English class. It truly changed my life, as I felt I had always carved my own path, even at a young age.

At age 23 I wrote my first screenplay titled Ashes to Ashes, about a police officer who enlists the help of a close friend to create a drug empire after his partner was gunned down during a drug raid. While I had no real knowledge of how to market my work, and living on the east coast, I tried a few query letters and continued to write. That same year I started writing my second screenplay, but as life and responsibility took over, I put my writing to the back burner and changed my priorities until recently. In December of 2013, I created a Facebook page to share my writing. Since that time, the Writer Jay Long page has attracted thousands of fans.

Story telling, expressing feelings through words and making people laugh are what I am best at. Hearing someone laugh feeds the soul and there is nothing like having someone use my words to help heal. Writing allows for the 'perfect' ending to any situation.

I enjoy connecting with fans and sharing pieces of myself with the world. I am following my dreams and traveling down a path that was laid out many years ago. I love hearing that others connect and can relate to my writing. I hope you follow me on one of or all of my social media accounts. I try and deliver more writing each day, as well as, recorded spoken versions of my more popular pieces. I also hope to start a blog series to help other upcoming writers with the many struggles they face when creating a platform as they continue following their dreams. Stay tuned.

Jay Long

Website : JayLongWrites.com
Facebook: WriterJayLong
Instagram: WriterJayLong
Twitter: JayLongWrites
YouTube: Jay Long Poetry
Pinterest: JayLongWrites
Tumblr: WriterJayLong
Email : jaylongwrites @ gmail.com

Read more of my story at
patreon.com/jaylong